AN INTRODUCTION TO INTERPERSONAL THEORY AND PSYCHOTHERAPY

Carlton Cornett, M.S.W.
Michael Kavur, D.O., M.Ed.

Ideas into Books®
WESTVIEW

Ideas into Books®
W E S T V I E W
P.O. Box 605
Kingston Springs, TN 37082
www.publishedbywestview.com

ISBN 978-1-62880-198-9

First edition, April 2020

Good faith efforts have been made to trace copyrights on materials included in
this publication. If any copyrighted material has been included without
permission and due acknowledgment, proper credit will be inserted in
future printings after notice has been received.

Front Cover Photo Credits:

Upper Row Left: Otto Allen Will, Jr., M.D. (1910-1993). Photo Courtesy of the
Austen Riggs Center.

Upper Row Right: Harry Stack Sullivan, M.D. (1892-1949). Courtesy of the
Washington School of Psychiatry.

Lower Row Left: Leston Havens, M.D. (1924-2011). Photo Courtesy of the
Harvard University School of Medicine.

Lower Row Right: Frieda Fromm-Reichmann, M.D. (1889-1957). Photo
Courtesy of the Collections of Peerless Rockville.

Printed in the United States of America on acid free paper.

FOR LEON LURIE, M.S.

(1915-2012)

Compassionate Analyst and Profound Teacher

Photo by Carlton Cornett

Welcome

For several years I have given an introduction on interpersonal theory and psychotherapy to fourth year psychiatric residents at the Vanderbilt University School of Medicine. Since 2019 I have been supervising the clinical work of Dr. Michael Kavur, a creative and thoughtful student of interpersonalism. For this year's introduction to the residents, Michael and I decided to create a short study guide.

This introduction contains a series of essays outlining salient points of the interpersonal perspective. Dr. Kavur begins this series with an essay on his experience as a student grappling with the various models of the human condition presented to physicians in the United States. It is, to me, a very interesting study of one physician's experience. I authored the remaining essays, focused on: general concepts, human development, psychopathology, and clinical work from an interpersonal viewpoint. The final paper may strike some readers as a little provocative, but an open-minded reading may challenge some to think outside the box about psychotherapy. Each essay is followed by a page where readers may record their thoughts and feelings about the previous material.

We hope you find these essays stimulating. If interpersonalism resonates with you, we wish you the best in the further study of this humanistic perspective on the psychological functioning of the person.

Carlton Cornett, LCSW
Nashville, Tennessee

Some Brief Definitions of Interpersonal Psychotherapy

Harry Stack Sullivan

"Psychotherapy is the inducing by chiefly verbal interchange of changes in the patient's living with significant others" (1949, p.9).

Hilde Bruch

"… a situation where two people interact and *try to come to an understanding of one another*, with the specific goal of accomplishing something beneficial for the complaining person" (1974, p. ix, italics added).

Marianne Horney Eckardt

"Another way of thinking about therapy is being in an on-going creative dialogue. The patient or the therapist suggests an idea or a story and the other responds … "Our 'wisdom' is good listening and reflecting on what we think we hear" (Rubin 2014, p. 117).

Leston Havens

"At any time all our responses reflect mixtures of fantasy and fact. The most commonplace stimulus sets off recollections, reminders, recognitions that make the present seemingly historical. The method of participant observation is centrally the method of bringing reality into this history-laden present" (1976, pp. 23-24).

Leon Lurie

"… the process of helping somebody know what they already know, though they don't know they know it." (2006)

"… there are two factors involved in getting help with self-destructive, persistent, ubiquitous patterns of thinking and acting. The first is a concerned therapist who has the skill to create a relationship enabling the participants to speak from the heart, i.e. to have a real 'conversation,' in contrast to the usual exchanges where strategy is the main concern. The second is the careful teasing out into the open of the … motives and attitudes that have been getting in the way of positive and nourishing ways of being with oneself and others." (2007)

CONTENTS

ONE

Learning Psychotherapy
Michael Kavur, D.O., M.Ed.

The Medical Model

All aspiring psychiatrists in Western medicine begin their training under the paradigm of the medical model – a rigorous set of procedures aimed at identifying causation and providing remediation of disease. During the first two years of my medical school training, I was inundated with learning the basic medical sciences, disease pathology and the clinical skills needed to arrive at a correct diagnosis and treatment. This was followed by two additional years of clinical training, which consisted of rotating through various medical specialties to further refine medical knowledge and skill sets. Throughout medical school, there were high stake checkpoints: medical boards, clinical proficiency exams, presenting on the wards or assisting in surgical procedures, to name a few. This rigorous process ensures that every graduate from a medical school is proficient in the medical model.

Residency serves as a time to practice serving as a physician in a specific field of medicine, a time to advance one's medical knowledge, practice new skill sets and ultimately grow in the confidence needed to practice medicine independently. At the onset of my intern year, I felt a considerable amount of unease when, for the first time, a patient addressed me as "doctor." I knew that with this revered title came a depth of responsibility I had never before held.

Fortunately, the four years of intense medical training paid off and I adapted to the new role. With each new patient encounter, my anxiety would rise and fall through the diagnostic and treatment process and a personal sense of satisfaction prevailed after fulfilling my role of doctor.

For me, the process was transforming – learning a paradigm that valued one based on his or her knowledge and ability to perform. Modern medical training produces competent physicians who are equipped to bring healing to the sick. However, as I began my psychiatric rotations in residency, the paradigm I assimilated was less than helpful. I was faced with fuzzy boundaries between normal and pathological, vast heterogeneity, a lack of specific biomarkers, and treatments with poorly defined mechanisms. My ability to perform under the medical model was severely restricted and so began my journey of learning the paradigm of psychiatry.

Towards a New Paradigm

Far from the predictable response of blood glucose levels to insulin or the biomarkers that measure heart failure, understanding the functions of behavioral systems is far more challenging. The mechanisms that regulate a person's self-esteem, mood or anxiety arise from a vast array of neural circuitry superimposed on a lifetime of experience, thus, greatly limiting modern science's ability to study and understand such processes. The DSM attempts to provide an organizational framework by capturing essential features of psychopathology but diagnoses do not map well onto the cognitive, circuit and genetic aspects of mental disorders, and can lead to oversimplified conceptualizations of psychiatric illness.

Without clear cause and effect relationships in psychiatry, diagnosis and treatment is much less definitive. For a physician trained under the medical model, this level of ambiguity was difficult to tolerate. I began questioning my value when, for many of my patients, I didn't have the medical knowledge to provide treatment. For the depressed, suicidal patient admitted to the inpatient unit for a time-limited hospitalization, I did not have solutions. I could start an antidepressant but knew full well it would take weeks before an effect might be evident. Interestingly, I saw many of these patients' suicidality resolve and depression remit before they discharged, but not because of any intervention I had offered – or so I thought.

I was unaware that other processes were occurring. The power of a kind smile, the comfort of companionship, the encouragement of a supportive word and the refuge of the therapeutic milieu was medicine in and of itself. An amorphous blend of nurses, mental health specialists, social workers, therapists and pharmacists, collectively working to create a safe and compassionate environment fostered healing. For the first time in my medical career, I had to relinquish control, admit to not knowing and rely on something other than pure medical knowledge to provide healing to my patients. I had to unlearn the medical model to get to the heart of psychiatry.

An Introduction to Psychotherapy

Practicing psychiatry requires acceptance of a certain degree of unknowing. There are conflicting theories concerning the etiology of diseases we treat – schizophrenia, depression, anxiety, and so on, and the mechanisms for many treatments remain a mystery. Fortunately, modern science is advancing quickly and new approaches in genetics, neuroscience and behavioral sciences show promise of elucidating the biology of mental illness. But for the time being, the majority of diagnostic and treatment decisions for psychiatric conditions are based on observational data rather than biological data.

One of the treatments in psychiatry – psychotherapy – has long roots going back hundreds, if not thousands of years. A little over one hundred years ago, Sigmund Freud developed psychoanalytic theory to explain human behavior, but as modern science emerged, his methods were not viewed as scientific. In the 1970s, a rift formed between psychiatry and psychology after the emergence of psychopharmacology. Emphasis was placed on a biological construct of mental illness and psychotherapy was dismissed as unscientific.

The pendulum has once again swung to the opposite pole and we now recognize that many of the neuroscience descriptions that once explained drug mechanisms are vastly over-simplified and that almost nothing we know about neurotransmitters and their receptors actually explains how psychotropic medications work. Furthermore, the concept of neuroplasticity – the ability for new neural pathways to form based on our everyday experiences – is now a generally accepted scientific truth. The human experience from birth onwards fundamentally interacts with our genetics to shape our behavior.

I became intrigued by the process of psychiatry and, in letting go of the strict medical model paradigm, felt free to explore new treatments in psychiatry that produced results, even if the mechanisms remain elusive. My formal training in psychotherapy began with cognitive behavior therapy (CBT). This orientation provided a structured approach to therapy; there were clear targets, progress could be measured and the process was time-limited. I read about modern brain imaging studies demonstrating positive changes after CBT, similar to those seen after SSRI administration. If there were any type of psychotherapy that would appeal to one with vestiges of the medical model, CBT certainly was the one.

Interestingly, as I spent more and more time practicing therapy, I noticed a trend develop. My curiosity about my patients often led me astray from the structured approach of CBT. The more I invested I became, the more the patient became a fellow person and less of a disease or disorder. As this shift occurred, a trust developed and my patients were instinctually drawn to explore their unhealthy way of managing life. They wanted to get better. I recognized that simply sitting with my patients with a genuine interest in their wellbeing was often more therapeutic than following a specific protocol. But the thorn in my side demanded evidence for my methods. I did not have a map to direct my sessions, nor objective scales to measure progress but my patients kept returning, reporting they felt better. I found myself searching for evidence to justify my methods (or lack thereof) and felt anxious at the least set back.

Learning Psychotherapy

Towards the end of my third year of residency, I began seeing one of my most complex therapy patients. "AJ" suffered from PTSD related to military sexual trauma, binge eating disorder, depression, and anxiety. Soon after my initial intake, I enthusiastically began preparing modules on binge-eating disorder, provided handouts and psychoeducation but she did not respond with equal engagement. Early into treatment, she asked me if I thought she should have bariatric surgery and I responded by asking if she could imagine herself being happy 100 pounds lighter. She reluctantly agreed that she would still feel depressed and acknowledged that her weight was merely a symptom. She had high expectations that her "doctor" would treat the core of her illness and provide the cure she needed.

Session after session AJ returned without feeling any better and my anxiety correspondingly increased because I felt like I should have the remedy. In subsequent visits, I initiated various medication trials to target her psychiatric symptoms but she experienced numerous side effects and eventually, during a two-week vacation from therapy, she quit taking them all. Out of desperation, I hypothesized various explanations for her behavior, attempted cognitive restructuring, and behavioral interventions but without much success. She kept returning feeling depressed, lonely, isolated and anxious.

Then she found out her husband had been having an affair and divorce proceedings soon followed. For months after, she spent each session venting her anger. For months, I simply provided a listening ear and attempted to supplement the "superego" that she was lacking. I felt like I wasn't doing anything in therapy other than investing my time. My anxiety soared because I did not have any clear theory or plan and I didn't perceive any improvement. It was around this time that I transitioned into my fourth year of residency and met with a new therapy supervisor, Carlton Cornett, LCSW. He introduced me to interpersonal psychotherapy, a theory I had little knowledge of, but after our first brief meeting, I knew this was what I was looking for.

A Departure from the Conventional

I read about the interpersonal concepts of self-disclosure, the one genus theorem, the tendency toward health, but most profound were my interactions with Carlton where he modeled many of these concepts. During one of my earlier sessions, he gave me a copy of his newly published book entitled *Being with Patients*. After reading through the book I was very impressed and during a supervisory session, complimented him on his publication and the many accomplishments he has had during his career. He paused a moment and replied that the comment made him feel anxious, that he has always had a hard time receiving compliments. This response was unexpected, but I experienced what it felt like to have an expert disclose his vulnerability. I couldn't explain the brain changes that made me feel more at ease but the experience drastically changed the dynamic between the two of us. He modeled that it was safe for me to express my vulnerabilities during supervision without fear of judgment and I have since excelled as a student of psychotherapy.

I wanted my patient to feel the same level of comfort I experienced with Carlton and eventually mustered up the courage to admit my own limitations to her. I told her I did not have the solution to her distress, that I really did not know what to do for her, but that I was willing to walk alongside her and maybe the two of us could figure things out. She just sighed a sense of relief when she heard this and we finally had a breakthrough. The next session she disclosed details of her abusive childhood and stated she never felt comfortable sharing this information before, even with her most intimate partners, for fear of shame or rejection. I was reminded of the words of Carlton, "It is the attempt to love and meet the need for intimacy which brings people to consult a psychotherapist," and wondered if this was what she had been looking for.

AJ went into detail about her unfortunate childhood, being raised in a family with all male brothers and cousins who never included her in any activities. Her father was physically abusive and struggled with numerous addictions and her mother was absent for the majority of the time. Her parents did not allow her to have friends outside of school and she remained significantly isolated. The only person that gave her attention was her sexually abusive uncle who molested her at the age of 11. When her loneliness was unbearable, she would return to him time and time again. She felt shameful, but the alternative was complete isolation and he was the only one who fulfilled her basic need for intimacy. She never told anyone about her past and has suffered ongoing shame, loneliness and isolation.

Carlton points out that, "Adjusting to loneliness is a lifetime task and many find themselves defeated in their attempts at this adjustment." AJ was taught from an early age not to have expectations for intimacy, but humans can't do well without it. During a low time in the midst of her divorce, AJ resorted to texting a man whom she just met on a dating site saying, "lets just fuck," in an attempt to have this need met. He politely responded stating she was not the type of girl he was looking for. As we processed this, AJ recognized an old, maladaptive pattern of behavior and gained insight into the origins of her lifelong interpersonal struggles.

Gradually, her freedom to respond to stressful situations expanded to include healthy and rewarding behavior. She resorted less to binge eating in times of stress, began reading bedtime stories to her children, and started exercising. Her mood and anxiety naturally improved. Carlton couldn't have summarized this process any more eloquently when he wrote, "intimacy provides the frame within which human transformation may occur and the origins of their problems snuffed out."

Reflections on What I've Learned

Without employing the concepts of interpersonal psychotherapy, I would have been left feeling anxious and frustrated by my lack of progress and direction with AJ. Learning about interpersonalism has transformed my approach to patients. I learned the power of modeling vulnerability and using self-disclosure as a way to engage my patients more as fellow persons and less as a disease or disorder. After admitting my limitations and engaging on an equal level with AJ, so many barriers broke down and the door opened to meaningfully begin the work of therapy. Patients come to therapy with the desire to get better – the tendency toward health. But all too often they are not permitted the safe space that fosters healing. I believe the core transformative process of interpersonalism is engaging in intimate relationships with our patients.

Carlton defines intimacy as "the need to know and to be known by another person." Intimacy creates a space in which rejection is unacceptable and mutual trust thrives. I personally cannot imagine anything but such a space in which I would feel comfortable to engage in meaningful therapy. Only under such conditions, can one begin to explore the depths of problems in living and communication. Intimacy dissolves loneliness and isolation, which Otto Will suggests is the root of psychopathology. Engaging in intimate relationships with patients provides an experiential model of how they can develop and sustain healthy relationships and overall better interpersonal functioning in their own personal lives.

Learning about interpersonalism has challenged my ideas of boundaries. In a way, I have pushed myself to the edge of my comfort zone, rather than staying well within the confines of a predetermined frame. I am struck by the truth of Ralph Waldo Emerson's statement that, "Men imagine that they communicate their virtue or vice only by overt actions, and do not see that virtue or vice emit a breath every moment." If we are not being honest with our patients, if we are not ready to engage in the intimacy that promotes a safe space for them to begin the transformative process, our patients will know it, and can we, as therapists, expect many gains?

Not every patient has the same goals and each person coming to therapy has vastly different needs. I certainly use tools I've learned from various theoretical orientations depending on the needs of my patients but operating from an interpersonal framework has vastly increased the possibility for transformation to take place. The process has been highly rewarding for me. Ample literature supports the notion that among the hundreds of different psychotherapeutic approaches, a few common factors – alliance, empathy and soliciting client feedback – are needed to maximize the effectiveness of therapy. The core of interpersonalism embodies these very principles.

Lifelong Learning

Unlearning the paradigm of the medical model and embracing a paradigm of psychiatry and further, psychotherapy, has been a long and difficult journey. Every now and then, my anxiety surges during sessions when I don't have a well-formulated plan, particularly during sessions when I take a passive role of simply listening. Doing something during a session is so much easier than doing nothing. But as I have grown, I recognize the notion of doing nothing during therapy is simply a fallacy.

Sometimes just sitting in a room listening to a patient as a fellow friend is the most powerful move a therapist can make.

I am thankful for the many supervisors who patiently listened to me week after week during my transformative journey in learning psychotherapy. I learned valuable insights along the way and am most thankful I stumbled across interpersonal psychotherapy. Psychotherapy does not come easily for those trained under the medical model but so much of the work that we, as medical doctors, do is about connecting with our patients and forming intimate bonds when our patients are at their most vulnerable. What better way to connect with our patients than to incorporate the ideas of interpersonalism.

Reflections

TWO

Core Assumptions of Interpersonalism
Carlton Cornett, M.S.W.

Harry Stack Sullivan, M.D.

Harry Stack Sullivan elicited diverse appraisals from those around him. Some were positive, others were not. His work, the foundation of the interpersonal viewpoint, was controversial. Today, his ideas pervade the field of mental health, largely without acknowledgement. Psychodynamic psycho-therapy, relational psychoanalysis, cognitive behavioral therapy (CBT), attachment-focused psychotherapies, and most other forms of the 'talking cure' owe unacknowledged debts to Sullivan.

Sullivan was the first empirically-oriented theorist. He was, as Richardson (1995) described Ralph Waldo Emerson – Sullivan's intellectual forbear – "... fascinated with the working of the scientific mind, with the nature of scientific knowledge, and with the strange union of precision and wonder in scientific inquiry" (p. 142). Sullivan (1953a) defined the subject matter of psychiatry as "... the study of interpersonal relations" (p. x), adding, "... I sought to segregate from everything else a disciplinary field in which operational methods could be applied with great practical benefits" (p. x). Observation was at the heart of his approach. If a phenomenon could not be observed, it might be inferred, but it could not be *known*. He (1953b) wrote,

Now at this point I wish to make a perduring distinction – a distinction that will be important from infancy to the end of living – between what can be observed by a participant observer, and what can never be so observed but must always be the result of inference from that which is observed. And this is the distinction between *overt processes* in interpersonal relations and *covert processes* (pp. 175-176, italics in the original).

Sullivan was also the first modern psychotherapeutic researcher. At the Sheppard and Enoch Pratt Hospital around 1927 Sullivan began to record psychotherapeutic sessions for later study. He initially did this through having his sessions taken down verbatim by a stenographer. Later, he used wax recordings to capture what occurred during sessions. The content of these sessions were studied by clinicians and professionals of other disciplines.

The Construction of Theories

Though Sullivan was always working toward pragmatically operationalizing concepts, it is important to understand the idiosyncrasies of psychological theory construction. He understood that a*ll theories of human nature are developed from subjective experiences.* Therefore, no theory can reasonably be expected to be universally applicable to every human being (Rubin 2014, p. 116). When discussing psychological theories, we are best served by the capacity to tolerate ambiguity, uncertainty, and a lack of finality. There is no last word on human psychology (Lurie 2008, pp. 173-174).

Every human being is a psychological theorist. Psychological theories are the way we organize the world and explain our thoughts, feelings, and actions to ourselves (Levenson 2018, p. 3). Such an organization also creates a narrative which offers the *potential* for understanding other people.

Interpersonalism proposes that our theories develop out of the necessity to understand and influence the actions and motivations of caregivers (Will 1971a, pp. 208-209; 1971b, p. 25). During the first weeks of life, the human infant is completely dependent on her caregivers, and probably does not differentiate herself from them. Within a relatively short period of time, however, she discovers that the primary caregiver is not an extension of herself. She learns this through the recognition that food does not appear simply because she is hungry, nor are other physiological or emotional needs satisfied immediately. This recognition is the rudimentary understanding that she must learn how to motivate caregivers to meet the basic needs of survival. The phrase 'emotional needs' is included above because it has been amply demonstrated that emotional interaction is necessary for intellectual and physical growth as well as basic survival (Sapolsky 2017, pp.188-192).

As we develop cognitively, our theories become more complex but often recede from awareness and are replaced by oversimplified convictions about "how people are." Formal psychological theories must have some common ground with our convictions about "how people are" to be considered seriously. Therefore, every formal psychological theory is personalized – and, thus, changed – by this personalization. As we then share the formal theory with others, we unwittingly share our personal revision of it. In her unpublished manuscript *Harry Stack Sullivan – the Man and His Part in a Professional Revolution: A Memoir*, Dorothy Blitsten (1966), a close friend of Sullivan, wrote:

> Almost inevitably, every person influenced by any man [or woman] understands only a part of what his mentor had in mind. Nevertheless, each tends to present the part as the whole and, in time, to overlook elaborations and accretions that are his own, not those of his teacher (p. i).

Otto Will (1963) noted that, "… in subscribing to a theory and technique, we commit ourselves – that is, our personalities become involved (often without our recognizing the fact) in the observations that we attempt to make" (p. 553). There is *no* psychological theory immune to this process, whether developed in a clinical or research setting. We ought to all bear in mind Harry Guntrip's (1971) admonition that, "To care for people is more important than to care for ideas, which can be good servants but bad masters" (p. 27).

A Philosophical Hybrid

Interpersonalism is a neo-Freudian theory of human development and functioning. Incorporating anthropology, linguistics, psychology, and sociology, it emphasizes interpersonal interactions rather than hypothesized intrapsychic phenomena. Interpersonalism is a philosophical hybrid of psychoanalysis and American pragmatism. It is as much in the lineage of Ralph Waldo Emerson, William James, Charles Cooley, and John Dewey as in the lineage of Freud. The pragmatic focus on observation and its emphasis on actions rather than metapsychology, differentiate interpersonalism from traditional psychoanalysis and give Sullivan's work a distinctive American tint. Besides Sullivan, other figures important in its development include Hilde Bruch, Frieda Fromm-Reichmann, Clara M. Thompson, and Otto Allen Will, Jr.

Sullivan's work paved the way for object-relations theory in the United Kingdom. Harry

Guntrip (1971), an important object-relations theorist, wrote, "… Harry Stack Sullivan's clear rejection of instinct as an adequate concept for human psychology, and his adoption of interpersonal relations experience as his basic concept, I believe as early as 1925, was the first absolute breakthrough of object-relations theory" (pp. 20-21). Both views of human nature remain closely interconnected, though object-relations theory has retained many of its Freudian roots, while interpersonalism has moved away from some key components of Freudian theory, including: human instincts, the oedipal conflict, use of the couch in clinical work, discounting a universally applicable *frame*, etc. (for a comprehensive list of Freudian theory that interpersonalists found objectionable, see Stern [2017], p. 11).

Nature of the Mind

There are core differences between traditional psychoanalysis and interpersonalism. Those core differences relate to the nature of the mind, the existence of the unconscious, and the conception of personal identity.

The classical psychoanalytic conception of *the mind* is of a closed system, located and contained *within* a person. Minds are considered, at their most basic level, to be independent units. The interpersonal conception of the mind emphasizes a more open and communal process, consisting of interconnected physiological and social processes and more *interactional* than individual. As Cooperman (1987) wrote, "Although the basic unit of biological functioning is the individual, the basic unit of psychological functioning seems always to be the twosome" (p.22; see also Stern 2017, pp. 18-19). Current interpersonal neurobiology also supports the Sullivanian conception of mind. "Both our internal neural functions and our shared communicative processes give rise to the process defined ... as mind" (Siegel 2015, p. 5). Clinically, this conception of the mind serves an important function in reminding us that, as Leston Havens (1989) wrote, "... discoveries are not made by separate minds, but spring up in the common space" (p. 25).

Identity, too, is not fixed, but dependent on the interpersonal context. It is fluid, changing as one's interpersonal situation changes. Like the mind, identity (*personality*, as well) *exists* in interpersonal interaction (though such interactions may be intrapsychic). Sullivan (1950) asserted that, "For all I know every human being has as many personalities as he has interpersonal relations ..." (p. 329).

Some traditional Freudian theorists have reduced the interpersonal position to the notion that there is no intrapsychic life, just as some interpersonalists have accused more traditional psychoanalysts of dismissing the interpersonal world. Interpersonal theory does not dispute that intrapsychic mentation occurs, but contends that intrapsychic processes can only be studied in interpersonal manifestations.

Finally, Sigmund Freud's psychoanalytic theory was constructed around the idea of a dynamic unconscious, maintained by repression, in which feelings, fantasies, experiences, and instincts reside. There is no clear concept of an unconscious in interpersonal theory (Levenson 2017, p. 158). Instead of repression, Sullivan relied on the concept of *selective inattention* or *dissociation*, which Otto Will (1962) defined as, "a dynamic system maintained by constant alertness to possibly disrupting events, and not a static situation in which ideas somehow lie fallow or inaccessible to experience" (p. 175). Stern (2017) writes:

> … unconsciousness is understood to be built into present-day relatedness. The expressions of the unconscious are configurations or patterns of relatedness, and they are not banished to the unconscious mind … but remain to be discovered in what is present but selectively inattended (p. 17).

Edgar Levenson (2018) defined dissociation as a process in which, "… the patient learns not to know what the patient knows she knows but is not supposed to know" (p. 165; see also Levenson 2017, p. 158). Some interpersonalists wonder whether or not the existence of an unconscious is beside the point. Sullivan (1950) wrote, "… the mind is phenomenologically coterminous with consciousness …" (p. 319). Experiences are either within or outside of awareness.

Mental Health

Sullivan (1953a) taught that, "*One achieves mental health to the extent that one becomes aware of one's interpersonal relations* …" (p. 207, italics in the original). He (1949) also wrote, "… the person who knows himself has mental health. He is content with his utilization of the opportunities that come to him. He values himself as his conduct merits. He knows and mostly obtains the satisfactions that he needs, and he is greatly secure [in his dealings with others]" (p. 9).

Mental Disorder

Sullivan (1953b) defined mental disorder as covering "… like a tent the whole field of inadequate or inappropriate performance in interpersonal relations" (p. 313). Interpersonal theory maintains that interpersonally ineffective patterns of behavior are learned through experiences with other people. Will (1975) asserted, "... we learn to be much of what we are" (p. 57). To some degree, every person experiences problems in living (Sullivan 1954, p. 17). Sullivan (1949) reminded students, "Everyone can and, at times, does show all the mechanisms that make up the functional psychoses" (p. 3). Sullivan battled the stigma surrounding mental disorder. He preferred the phrase, "problems in living" to "psychopathology" (Kay 2012, p. 20).

Just as ineffective patterns of learning begin in human relationships, more effective patterns can be learned in the psychotherapeutic relationship. The clarification of such ineffective patterns and their replacement with new learning is the focus of interpersonal psychotherapy.

Security

A central tenet of any theory of human nature is *motivation*. Why do we do what we do? In a single word, interpersonalism proposes that human beings are motivated by the desire for *security* (Kay 2012, p. 18). In the sense used here, security refers to a state devoid of anxiety. To achieve security, a person must have basic survival needs (food, water, shelter) met, but also subjectively feel her or himself to have value (self-esteem) in the eyes of those important to her or him.

Integral to security is an interpersonal milieu in which one can feel accepted as a person among persons. Security therefore involves a yearning for relationships, with the highest form of relationship being *intimacy*. Intimate relationships are those in which we have learned through experience that we may be safely vulnerable. Intimate relationships are reciprocal. Each person in the relationship can reveal aspects of her or himself that are "dangerous" (i.e. that have been previously rejected) without fear of similar rejection. This is what most human beings seek in a variety of effective and ineffective ways.

Anxiety

Anxiety is a key component of interpersonal theory. It is the experience, or expectation, of having one's actions judged as unacceptable, unlovable, or inhuman. Sullivan (1953b) wrote, "… anxiety in relatively adult people can often be explained plausibly as anticipated unfavorable appraisal of one's current activity" (p. 113). He (1950) also referred to anxiety as, "… what keeps us from noticing things which would lead us to correct our faults" (p. 327).

Anxiety is avoided by controlling awareness (i.e. selective inattention) and withdrawal from others. Withdrawal from human contact, however, results in loneliness, a feeling almost as terrible as anxiety. Writing in *The Washington Post*, Otto Will asserted,

"Psychiatry might be defined in part as the study of human loneliness and isolation. A common characteristic of so many of us in the world today is our guarded behavior with other human beings – as if we did not dare look closely at ourselves or our associates" (p. B5).

The Tendency toward Health

Sullivan (1954) held the belief, "… that every human being, if he has not been … demoralized by a long series of disasters, comes fairly readily to manifest processes which tend to improve his efficiency as a human being, his satisfactions, and his success in living – a tendency which I somewhat loosely call *the drive toward mental health*" (p. 100, italics in the original). One of Sullivan's closet colleagues was a German analyst named Frieda Fromm-Reichmann. She was director of psychotherapy at Chestnut Lodge, the first hospital dedicated to treating schizophrenic patients. She (1950) maintained that human beings are always capable of change, and "No doubt every human being has an innate tendency toward health, both mental and physical, just as one has a tendency toward fluid intake when thirsty and toward the intake of food when hungry" (p. 57).

The One-Genus Theorem

It is impossible to grasp Harry Stack Sullivan's point of view without understanding the central concept known as *The One-Genus Theorem*. It appears in the work of Sullivan's most important mentor, William Alanson White. In his *Autobiography of a Purpose*, White (1938) wrote:

> Instead of being very different from the rest of us [patients] are very much like the rest of us. ... I often say, much to the surprise of my listener as a rule, that some of the best friends I have ever had have been patients in hospitals for mental disease; and the reason that the listener is surprised by such a remark is because he has a conception of mental disease that makes such a thing impossible and makes the mentally ill person so different from the normal person in every way that the concept of friendship with him is inconceivable (p. 218; please note the use of the words, *friends* and *friendship*).

Sullivan described the One-Genus Theorem in multiple ways throughout his work. The clearest was his (1953b) simple assertion that "We shall assume that *everyone is much more simply human than otherwise* ..." (p. 32, italics in the original; see also 1953a, p. 16). Will (1980) wrote, "... the human being, no

33

matter how grossly disordered he may become, shares to varying degrees in the griefs and pleasures of each of us; in his 'sickness,' or his 'wickedness,' or 'depravity,' he retains his human status" (p. 161).

For psychotherapy to be helpful to the patient, the therapist must enter the relationship with the conviction that, "… this person sitting opposite me in my consulting-room is what I am" (Symington 2006, p. 79). Otto Will (1965) emphasized that "… the patient must become a person; he cannot remain a 'case' of dementia praecox or anything else" (p. 25). Will (1987) summarized his understanding of the One Genus Theorem as meaning, "… that there is no way out – no escape from the state of being human. Whatever we call our faults or virtues … we cannot be more, less, or otherwise than human" (p. 245; see also 1989, p. 137).

Developmental Periods

Interpersonal theory proposes six developmental periods. These periods are psychosocial, rather than psychosexual in nature (Levenson 2017, p. 160). They are epigenetic -- each builds on capacities or deficits developed in the previous period(s) (Will 1970a, p. 20). Developmental periods are not defined by age (though physiological maturation appropriate to each period must exist) but are focused on the development of specific interpersonal skills. This brief overview of a complex conception of human functioning is not intended to give more than an outline of central concepts.

Infancy: The period designated as Infancy begins at birth and ends with the development of *expressive speech* – though not necessarily words (Levenson 2017, p. 160). The primary task of infancy is the initial organization of perceptions of the self and others.

Childhood: Childhood extends from the development of speech to the need for playmates outside the home. The child begins to learn behavior judged by the culture as acceptable and unacceptable. During this process of enculturation the use of deception also develops to avoid disapproval and, thus, anxiety. It is in childhood that the subjective view of the self may be hidden from others, creating a personal and interpersonal dichotomy.

The Juvenile Period: The developmental task of the juvenile period is the establishment of relationships with peers. Such relationships require interpersonal skills such as cooperation, negotiation, boundary setting, and compromise.

Pre-Adolescence: This period extends from the need for friends to the development of one emotionally intimate relationship with a peer. Such a person is often called "a best friend" (Sullivan used the term, "chum"). Intimacy requires the ability to both reveal aspects of oneself and to accept the revelations of another. The pre-adolescent views herself as part of a world of relationships and "we" joins "I" as an important concept.

Adolescence: A priority during this period is the integration of sexuality into the concept of the self and other people. Along with intimacy, this integration signals the ability for loving, reciprocal, and sexually satisfying relationships.

Adulthood: Adult tasks include expanding the capacity for intimacy, establishing loving relationships, and accepting ambivalence, uncertainty, and mortality. Intimacy and love include the capacity for self-revelation appropriate to the level of depth in different relationships.

The acceptance of uncertainty, includes the acceptance of ourselves as imperfect human beings. As Emerson wrote in *Self-Reliance*, "There is a time in every man's education when he arrives at the conviction that envy is ignorance; that imitation is suicide; that he must take himself for better, for worse, as his portion ..." Similarly, the acceptance of uncertainty precludes expectations of perfection, both of ourselves and others. It also includes the attempt to view the world in hues of gray rather than in reductionistic black and white (Will 1970a, p. 22). As Otto Will (1987) asserted, "Attendant upon hope is disappointment; to dare one is to risk the other" (p. 249).

William Butler Yeats (1902) wrote in *'The Untiring Ones'*: It is one of the great troubles of life that we cannot have any unmixed emotions. There is always something in our enemy that we like, and something in our sweetheart that we dislike. It is this entanglement of moods which makes us old, and puckers our brows and deepens the furrows about our eyes.

Yeats described the difficulty of ambivalence and the reasons that we seek to avoid recognizing that it encompasses our relational lives. The most common manifestation of the attempt to avoid the experience of ambivalence is through *splitting* – the alternating perception of ourselves and others and their actions in absolute terms (See also Will 1970a, p. 22; for a further description of the relationship between ambivalence and adult maturity see Levenson 2018, p. 62; Searles 1979, p.480).

Finally, the acceptance of mortality is the acceptance that all life ends, including our own. Within this acceptance, we search for meaning and purpose. We accept that love and loss are inherently entwined and inseparable.

In the foregoing pages an attempt has been made to describe important assumptions of the interpersonal tradition. As has been emphasized, no single theory is universally applicable nor universally explanatory. However, interpersonalism provides both an accessible and pragmatic means of thinking psychodynamically about those people who we call patients and who repose their trust in us.

Reflections

THREE

Some Origins of 'Problems in Living'

Carlton Cornett, M.S.W.

Fractured Relationships

In the interpersonal tradition, *psychopathology is viewed as learned interpersonal actions that interfere in developing and sustaining relationships, particularly intimate relationships.* Though there are a myriad of ways that psychopathology may be displayed, it is often most evident in anxiety, troubled communication, and restrictions in awareness.

Anxiety is the central phenomenon behind all interferences in interpersonal functioning. One avoids the direct pursuit of need satisfaction because of anxiety that revelation of the need will be found unacceptable and that rejection, shame, or loneliness will result.

Communication

A troubled human being often employs unclear communication. William Alanson White (1938), Sullivan's most important psychiatric influence, wrote, "I have always said that clear thinking involved the capacity of clear expression, that if a person could not tell a thing so that someone else could understand it, it was because he did not understand it himself …" (p. 176). Unclear communication may involve an incomplete or disorganized understanding of the topic, particularly when it appears around emotions, memories, or descriptions of interpersonal events. When communication is opaque, it allows the troubled person to keep secrets from herself or her listener.

During the years that Sullivan worked with people diagnosed as schizophrenic, he "... observed that they often used language more as a means of defense than of communication; their speech served to keep people at a distance, thus protecting an already low self-esteem" (Will 1954, p. xiii). The same can be true for all of us. An observant therapist can gauge the level of anxiety in the room by noting the prevalence of abstraction and ambiguity in the conversation. *Clear communication is a goal of psychotherapy because obscurity and opacity prevent connection based on mutual understanding.*

Restrictions in awareness, the result of selective inattention, create narratives with "holes" that are glossed over and *scotoma* ("blind spots") that do not allow of other possible hypotheses or explanations. Such defenses help the patient maintain a seemingly coherent narrative that avoids vulnerability, but leaves the listener disconnected because what she hears often feels vaguely untrue or contrived.

A Theory of Psychopathology

For centuries, medical practitioners, shaman, and mental health professionals have debated the cause(s) of mental illness. Some have viewed it as the result of physiological dysfunction; others as a result of divinity or near-divinity. With the advent of psychoanalysis, the human environment in which a child is cared for (or otherwise) and in which that child functions as an adult have been increasingly emphasized. As a general hypothesis, we currently believe that both physiology (including genetics) and the human environment play substantial roles in the development of problems in living.

For interpersonalism, nature and nurture are balanced in this way: genetic and physiological potentialities are facilitated or obstructed by developmental experiences. Sullivan (1953b) wrote:

> It is ... clear that the inborn potentialities which thus mature over a term of years are remarkably labile, subject to relatively durable change by experience, and antithetic to the comparatively stable patterns to which the biological concept of *instinct* applies (p. 21, italics in the original).

Complete Dependence: The First six Months

Sullivan (1953b) hypothesized six epigenetic developmental periods, the earliest being infancy (p. 33; see above). Infancy encompasses the period of birth to eighteen months. *Functionally, Infancy is the period of absolute dependence, ending with the development of rudimentary expressive speech.*

The human being is born with a variety of needs that create physiological tensions, the vast majority of which cannot be quelled without the cooperation of a caregiver. Such cooperation Sullivan (1953b) called *tenderness* (p. 59). The infant must be fed and hydrated; caregivers must ensure a survivable temperature, must protect the infant from danger, and must clean the infant to prevent both discomfort and infection.

Otto Will (1963) defined *need* as a requirement of the organism, "… which prompts to action" (p. 1). Without symbolic, expressive speech, the infant has multiple needs but a limited number of actions with which to engage the caregiver. Therefore, to satisfy a need or reduce the tension of it, the infant *acts* in the only way available to her – engaging the caregiver in addressing, hopefully satisfying, the need. Such engagement involves vocalizations (e.g. screaming), affective displays (e.g. crying), and body movements (e.g. facial expressions). Caregiver empathy is also necessary to establish successful patterns of tenderness.

During Infancy, the reliability of caregiver responsiveness forms the rudimentary elements of a *worldview*. A sense of reliability or lack thereof in meeting her needs predisposes the infant to view the world as *satisfying* or *frustrating*. This view is very similar to Erik Erikson's (1982) conception of the psychosocial crisis, 'Basic Trust vs. Basic Mistrust' (p. 32). When a view of the world as unsafe or frustrating has been strengthened by subsequent experiences, one of the primary goals of psychotherapy is providing a space for safe dependence; Otto Will (1975) wrote, "Dependency with security is a necessary preliminary to relationship and independence" (p. 63).

Six to Eighteen Months: Differentiation & Origins of the Self

Around six months, the infant develops – again, in rudimentary form – an awareness of being separate from the primary caregiver. Sullivan proposed that the infant's differentiation of herself from the primary caregiver (mother) begins with the infant's realization that the nipple is not always immediately responsive to her need. He (1953a) wrote, "The clarification of the nipple as borne by another person instead of its being a relatively unmanageable part of one's own cosmic entity is the first step in shrinking to life size" (p. 33).

From this clarification, the infant becomes aware that the primary caregiver's body is "not my body" (Sullivan 1953b, p. 161). Sullivan contended that, as the infant differentiates the nipple as "not my body," she begins to evaluate the nipple as "good" and "bad." The good nipple is readily responsive and satisfies the infant's need for food.

The bad nipple frustrates because it is not immediately responsive or is withdrawn before complete satisfaction. The infant develops a rudimentary understanding that the nipple is not a part of her, but is more or less responsive to her needs. This understanding then expands to a recognition that her actions play a role in the satisfaction of her needs.

With the understanding that her actions determine, to some extent, the availability of the nipple, *personifications of the nipple are gradually transformed into personifications of the self. Good Me* are those actions which result in need satisfaction and approval from caregivers. The smile, tickle, and the satisfaction of physiological needs form the basis of Good Me, which will be expanded, contracted, and otherwise refined throughout life.

The lack of need satisfaction and inferred disapproval from the caregiver(s) prompts the infant to hide the actions that are *presumed* to have elicited the negative response; thus, the personification Bad Me is formed. In this process of the development of Good Me and Bad Me, is the earliest form of what can be referred to as *splitting*. As the infant grows, she attempts to hide Bad Me from herself and others. Splitting is one of the precursors to selective inattention (which is mastered in the juvenile developmental period).

The final component of the self, developed through what Sullivan called *foresight* (learning the often-predictable consequences of one's actions on others) is *Not Me*. Not Me is created as the infant's actions call forth overwhelming anxiety in the caregiver(s). The anxiety is experienced as destructive and potentially threatening to existence itself. Any actions calling forth such anxiety must be disavowed *as if* they do not exist. They are then dissociated. That, of course, does not mean that the qualities embodied in those actions cease to exist. They return in instances of deep anxiety, when we do something, we thought ourselves incapable of, confusing and disorienting ourselves and those around us.

Misattunement & Misattribution

For a variety of reasons, the infant may have difficulty engaging the caregiver in addressing her needs (e.g. as needs become more complex, signaling actions may lag behind). Caregivers may also be misattuned, distracted, or otherwise unable to decipher the infant's signals.

Misattunement is the process in which infant and caregiver's perceptions are dystonic. Misattunement confuses the infant, and, if chronic, the infant may become misattuned to herself. Additionally, if the infant senses no correlation between her actions and the responses of caregivers, she may attempt novel actions (e.g. frowning rather than smiling). These actions may either be more communicative (i.e. growth) to caregivers or more confusing (i.e. an impediment to attunement). If caregivers become more confused, then responsiveness may become even more unreliable.

Misattunement generally leads to *misattribution*. Misattribution is the caregiver's response to an infant's need as if it were another need or to a feeling as if it were another feeling "Oh, baby is hungry" may become "It's time for baby's nap." Also called *mystification*, it is "… the teaching of the child to disbelieve his own perceptions" (Will 1972, p. 86). Edgar Levenson (2018) described misattribution or mystification as, "… the gap between what is said and what is shown" (p. 173).

Sustained misattribution is more often involved with caregiver psychopathology (especially selective inattention). Chronic misattribution can lead to a perception in the infant that she is unknowable and, over time, is hypothesized to be a factor in schizophrenia (Will 1968, p. 568). "If I see something and someone tells me that I am wrong, that the thing is not there, or if I feel something but someone tells me that I am feeling something else, it is capable of driving me mad" (Symington 2006, p. 17).

Anxiety

The infant learns to seek security when afflicted by the tension of anxiety. Without language, the tension of anxiety is difficult to communicate to caregiver(s) because it does not involve a single, tangible element for satisfaction. The infant may try to reduce anxiety by sucking at the breast, though not hungry, or masturbation, perhaps increasing anxiety in caregiver(s).

This begins the lifelong search for security. If caregivers are reliable *enough* in soothing the infant's anxiety, she is believed to experience what later can be called self-esteem and personal agency. If a pattern of unreliable response to her anxiety develops, then such anxiety may begin to be unrecognized (e.g. experienced as anger), unattended to (e.g. "medicated" with various substances), and confused with somatic processes.

The Self-System or Self-Dynamism

Early experiences of anxiety create the self-system or self-dynamism, an early warning system which detects potential situations that may involve anxiety and focuses on keeping potential threats out of awareness, through selective inattention – denial, dissociation, projection, etc. These defenses are interpersonal in nature, akin to interpersonal manipulation. As such, they often frustrate or anger others and interfere in the development or continuation of relationships. Psychotherapy focuses heavily on expanding the boundaries of awareness to free-up problem-solving capabilities. This is what some analysts refer to as "defense analysis."

Loneliness

During the separation involved in creating the self, the infant experiences a sense of separateness and distance. This is the beginning of loneliness. *Adjusting to loneliness is a lifetime task and many find themselves defeated in their attempts at this adjustment.* Otto Will (1949) suggested that psychiatry "… might be defined in part as the study of human loneliness and isolation" (p. B5).

Loneliness can be transformed into a sense of non-existence or a sense of being viewed with indifference. Some symptoms that develop from the fear of non-existence and perceived indifference can mimic the delusions of schizophrenia (and may account for some aspects of this disorder).

Stephen Grosz (2013) recently proposed that "paranoia" may be a defense against the catastrophe of non-existence. He wrote:

> In other words, paranoid fantasies are disturbing, but they are a defence. *They protect us from a more disastrous emotional state – namely, the feeling that no one is concerned about us, that no one cares.* The thought 'so-and-so

has betrayed me' protects us from the more painful thought 'no one thinks about me' (p. 83, italics added).

He continued, referring to a patient who believed that she was the target of a terrorist or terrorist organization.

The thought 'someone wants to kill me' gave her an experience of being hated – but not forgotten. She existed in the mind of of the terrorist. *Her paranoia shielded her from the catastrophe of indifference* (p. 85, italics added).

Neville Symington (2012), an object relations theorist, wrote, "A patient said to me: 'I think Descartes had it wrong. It is not 'I think therefore I am' but '*You* think therefore I am.' The belief here is that one person thinking about the other brings about the birth of I" (p. 3, italics in the original).

Final Thoughts

In this essay, the authors have attempted to offer a metaphorical model for the development of psychopathology using the developmental period called infancy. Though difficulties can develop in any period, they will likely be related to patterns developed in infancy. It is from this age that the most deeply troubling symptoms arise and are most difficult to ameliorate. Indeed, it would seem that, during this period, the spark of human vitality can either be nurtured into a flame or very nearly snuffed out.

Reflections

FOUR

Sullivan's Challenge:
Love in Psychotherapy

Carlton Cornett, M.S.W.

A Theory of Love

In his 1817 *Biographia Literaria*: the poet, Samuel Taylor Coleridge, wrote, "... there have been men in all ages who have been impelled as by an instinct to propose their own nature as a problem, and who devote their attempts to its solution." Put another way, we look at our own lives to describe human nature. Sigmund Freud did so and so, too, did Harry Stack Sullivan.

Harry Stack Sullivan had a theory of love. It is not especially dreamy or romantic -- not one that inspires thoughts of warm hearths and staring into a lover's eyes. In fact, Charles McCabe of the *San Francisco Chronicle* admiringly called it, "... a cold-blooded definition of what I felt could not be defined" (Will 1981). I think that it is a visionary definition that captures a quality of love that may be a little uncomfortable because it asks much of us. In a 1981 paper presented at The Sheppard and Enoch Pratt Hospital, Otto Will, Sullivan's patient and student between 1946 and 1949, noted that Sullivan's definition requires qualities that are, "... not easy to attain."

Loving

In *Conceptions of Modern Psychiatry* (1953a), Sullivan wrote, "When the satisfaction or security of another person becomes as significant to one as is one's own satisfaction or security, then the state of love exists. So far as I know, under no other circumstances is a state of love present, regardless of the popular usage of the word" (pp. 42-43). This definition emphasizes *giving* love. Love exists when the satisfaction of another person's needs and the emotional security of another person are as important to me as is my own.

Sullivan (1953b) believed that intimacy is a ubiquitous human need, though it can be stunted by experiences that result in poor self-esteem, rejection, and anxiety. He described intimacy as the need to know and to be known by another person. This is not meant as an absolute. Knowledge of ourselves and others can never be complete and that is the foundation of the loneliness that haunts every human life, whether it be for a moment, a year, or a lifetime. Sullivan taught that the need for intimacy can only be satisfied when one is vulnerable enough to reveal major portions of the self to another, risking rejection for those aspects deemed unacceptable or unlovable. Satisfaction of the need for intimacy also involves the capacity to accept another's revelations of human imperfections. It is in the attempt to love and meet the need for intimacy which brings people to consult a psychotherapist (Sullivan 1953b, pp. 290-296; Will 1970b, p. 3).

Love in Psychotherapy

Otto Will (1971a) described being challenged by a patient to think about the role of love in psychotherapy. He wrote, "Some years past I said to a patient that, in my opinion, love was not in itself a curative agent. The reply was – with emphasis: '*You are very likely wrong.*'" Will discounted love as "… an elusive and ephemeral phenomenon, for the most part private and poorly comprehended" (p. 16).

In a later paper, entitled "On 'Caring' in Psychotherapy", given at Chestnut Lodge in Rockville, Maryland, Will (1979b) returned to the subject of love. He reiterated Sullivan's definition, but added that the inclusion of the word "almost" (When the satisfaction or security of another person becomes *almost* as significant …), which makes Sullivan's definition less perfectionistic and more attainable. He also reported another challenge to his view of the place of love in therapy. He was working with a woman who made a serious suicide attempt and was hospitalized. He told the group:

> As she was partly conscious and I came to see her in the hospital, she asked me if I cared about her and I said, 'Yes, I did.' And she asked me if I loved her. I felt embarrassed by that question and hesitated some and did not know quite what to say,

but later I was able to answer and say, 'Yes, I did.'

What I found on recorded interviews with Will were other instances of him discussing love in psychotherapy. It is clear that he understood love, as Sullivan defined it, to play a key role in the process. Barton Evans (1996) has also pointed out the centrality of love to Sullivan's clinical work. He wrote, "While Sullivan rarely used the word love in his writings, his work strongly implies that it is love between humans which ultimately liberates us" (p. 20).

Love at Sheppard Pratt Hospital

The first expression of Sullivan employing love in psychiatric care occurred on his unit at the Sheppard and Enoch Pratt Hospital in Towson, Maryland. The unit, which began operation between 1926 and 1928, was, at best, unconventional. Sullivan (1962) wrote that each patient was treated "… as a *person among persons*" (p. 285, italics in the original). The unit staff was composed of "overt homosexuals" (i.e. openly gay men) and they were encouraged to share experiences and feelings about their sexuality with the patients, discuss affection, and touch appropriately (i.e. non-sexually). There remains some mystery as to whether there were incidents of sexual interaction.

Whether inappropriate touching occurred or not, Otto Will (1983) captured the intent of the unit: "Sullivan believed that patients surrounded by affection and intimacy rather than hate or humiliation are better able to reorganize their personalities and that the patients' social environment and what they learn from their communal experience contribute a great deal to recovery" (p. viii).

It is in this description of the Sheppard Pratt Unit that an outline of Sullivan's later clinical emphases is apparent. First, Sullivan believed that self-esteem or self-respect is a key component of the human personality. As Will pointed out, the atmosphere of the unit was "affection and intimacy." As Sullivan would later assert, intimacy is reached when mutual self-revelation occurs. In this regard, Sullivan was an active member of the milieu. He engaged in self-disclosure, sometimes revealing deeply personal aspects of his thoughts, feelings, and experiences. In one interaction a patient searchingly questioned, "... I wouldn't let any man I couldn't trust sleep with me – would you?" Sullivan replied, "I have let men I did not trust sleep with me – yes" (Wake 2006, p. 334).

Will also captures Sullivan's belief that, given a safe and affirming environment, patients have an inherent tendency toward growth (see above).

Finally, Will highlights Sullivan's belief that new experience (i.e. new learning) should be the focus of the clinician's work.

Creating a Loving Environment

We cannot decide that the patient will *feel* loved. We cannot expect the patient to experience our actions in any particular way. It is important to be alert to patients' willingness to comply with *our* wishes and needs, and to our own comfort in allowing them to do so. If helpful, therapy is a process constantly informed by observation, discussion of those observations. Balanced with this understanding is a desire to aid our patients in acquiring new experiences -- new learning that will compete with previously learned ways of interacting with others -- some of which may be interfering in obtaining satisfaction in their relationships.

The primary tool of the psychotherapist is clarification of what is happening here and now. Often, clarification takes the form of questions such as: how is my presence contributing to the patient's experience? We cannot know at the outset, but we can ask. In short, the therapeutic relationship is the simultaneous repetition of old patterns to be clarified and a "space" in which to experiment with new ways of being in relationships. If the therapist approaches the relationship in this way, she or he will grow, too.

Being "On the Patient's Side."

David Rioch (1985), one of Sullivan's closest friends and colleagues, wrote that Sullivan, "... was on the patient's side, first and last" (p. 145). Sullivan sometimes demonstrated this by simply sitting next to a patient. They would gaze together in silence or reconstruct the experiences of a patient's life as if on a screen in front of them. Incidentally, this is one of the ways that Sullivan dealt with transference. As he and the patient sat together, they would clarify the patient's feelings as each important character appeared on the screen. He offered no interpretations, but waited for the patient to recognize affective patterns in her or his relationships (1979, p. 26). Leston Havens (1989) described employing the same practice of sitting beside patients. He wrote, "It represented the spatial statement of a psychological fact: I am on your side, we look out together, our search for trouble is more in the world out there than in you as solitary being" (p. 52).

"Being on the patient's side," however, is much more complex than where the therapist sits. For some patients, sitting beside them might feel intrusive, not at all enhancing their security. Being on the patient's side is potentially demonstrated in a variety of ways. One is the therapist's transparent conviction that "We're in this relationship *together*." Several times over the course of his interviews with

Kim Chernin, a psychotherapist in San Francisco and author of *A Different Kind of Listening* (1995), Otto Will recounted a memory of Sullivan that clearly had an impact on him. He remembered that a good friend was also in therapy with Sullivan. Though he did not reveal the exact nature of his friend's circumstances, he made it clear that his friend was somewhat desperate. I assume that his friend told Will of the following interaction that occurred at the end of one session with Sullivan.

Sullivan said, "Doctor, I sure would like to give you a helping hand. But, right now, I don't know how. So I guess that we just have to totter along *together.*" Will added, "And my friend said that was very encouraging." ... Will then commented, "[The] therapist doesn't have to be a great success, [the] therapist just has to *be* there" (K. Chernin interview of O.A. Will, March 31, 1992; see also Will 1989, p. 140). Most of all, Sullivan was *present.*

"Being on the patient's side" is the product of trial and error, observation and discussion. It will be different in each therapeutic dyad. On one occasion, a patient I (CC) had seen for several years, was distraught because he had gotten up in the middle of the night and, still partially asleep, knocked over a piece of china which broke when it hit the floor. During his next session, he was enraged with himself, calling himself, "stupid," "clumsy," etc.

After listening a few minutes, I just shared a simple thought: "Maybe a natural part of being a piece of china is breaking." I could have interpreted his perfectionism, the harshness of his self-condemnation, but did not. He would have understood such an interpretation, but not, at least in my estimation, experientially. My goal was simply to remind him that certain ends are determined by factors outside of our control. My comment seemed to free him a little from his relentless responsibility for the imperfections of his life. I have been surprised how often he has returned to that comment saying, "You remember what you said about china, well I discovered this week that a natural part of being a tire is going flat," etc. My understanding of what occurred is that I had been on his side – and it stuck. I have discovered over the years that, for me, being on the patient's side is often communicated non-verbally.

In a recent session with a woman that I (CC) have seen for nearly five years, once to twice weekly, she began telling me about a conflict with a sibling who can be very abusive. As she began to tell me about the most recent conflict, particularly what the sibling had said, I rolled my eyes.

She stopped, smiled, pointed at me and said "Yes, that's it, you're exactly right!"

I asked, "What am I exactly 'right' about?"

She responded, "I'm tired of being yelled at by [the sibling] and Goddamnit, I'll hang up the next time [the sibling] does it!" She has followed through on that course of action.

Let me emphasize that I wasn't sure what I was communicating with the eye roll, though it felt right. If my eye-roll had communicated that I was bored, impatient, frustrated, found her complaints without merit, etc., then we would have examined what we both knew about eye-rolling. The same is true of broken china. However, on these two occasions, I landed on the patient's side. I find that it is very difficult to know if I will be on the patient's side until I do or say something and then we look at it.

Respecting the Patient

Sullivan (1954) called respect part of the "expertise" of psychotherapy. He taught that:

> ... respect for you, which is so impressive when experienced, not only takes the general form of endorsing your worth as a companion in the same room, but is also shown by a certain warning of any severe jolts that you might receive in the discussion ... In other words, you are well managed, first, when you are treated as worth the trouble, and second, when the other person is keenly aware of, and

sensitive to, disturbances in your feeling of personal worth, in your security, while in his presence (pp. 28-29).

Respect can be demonstrated in various ways. Chiefly, it occurs when we monitor the anxiety in the room, both ours and the patient's. It also occurs when we accept responsibility for our anxiety and acknowledge its effect on our actions.

Attending to Signs of Anxiety

Sullivan recognized that new learning could not take place when anxiety was too great. And it is new learning, new experience, that the interpersonal therapist seeks to provide the patient. Sullivan was attentive to the security of his patients. He would offer a choice of paths during anxious moments, with ambiguous statements like, "Your mother was not an unmitigated blessing." The patient could then choose whether to explore "unmitigated" or "blessing" (Havens 1989, p. 52). A young gay man recently told me (CC) of his first love. He described this partner as having opened a new, more positive view of himself (the patient) but had devastated him when he left. I responded to this ambivalent description with an ambiguous statement, offering a choice of directions: "Thank God for that son of a bitch."

It is equally important that the therapist attend to her or his own anxiety. Anxiety in the therapist, activated by interactions with the patient, is broadly thought of as countertransference in this tradition. Countertransference is, of course, not only unavoidable, but an aid to the process.

In a session with a very anxious woman who had just learned that she was pregnant, I (CC) found myself feeling increasingly anxious. Her thinking was catastrophic and she was describing her many fears and worries; we were about halfway through the session. She stopped for a moment and I said, "I'm feeling really anxious – thinking about the next eight months and the ways that I may not know how to help." Having given voice to my anxiety and, remembering Will's memory of Sullivan and his friend, I then added, "But I guess I don't need to know all the answers, I just need to be here."

She said, "I promise I won't expect you to know all about being pregnant."

I responded, "So, maybe we can both relax a little, this is the first time for both of us."

She said, "I guess I don't have to know all about it either."

I then called her attention to the way that she nurtured me and then herself.

Her ability to manage her own anxiety surfaced in responding to my anxiety and then – perhaps for just the rest of that session – she was aware that she *could* manage her anxiety. One of the goals of psychotherapy was accomplished, her awareness was expanded. Another was also achieved: she experienced my imperfection. As we discussed this, I learned that her perfectionistic mother would not have accepted responsibility for her anxiety, but instead, told the patient, "Stop it, you're making me anxious!" My anxiety was about perfectionism, too -- that I must have the answers. So, we enacted a transference/countertransference pattern, but resolved it in a different way. It turned out that neither of us needed to be perfect.

It seems that what we call transference and what we call countertransference are inseparable, ubiquitous, and always constructed upon each other -- two lifetimes of experience intermingling, sometimes colliding, in a hopefully safe space. As Will (1979a) wrote, "In a sense the patient shows to us not only himself but a view of *our* world and *our* living in it (p. 564, italics in the original; see also Will 1971b, p. 37). We, in turn, do the same for our patients.

Effective Communication

This brings us to the idea of intimacy, the essential feature of which is to know and be known

71

by another person. Hopefully, we would all agree that communication – both verbal and non-verbal – offers the greatest possibility for accomplishing this goal. However, we would probably also all agree that we use communication – especially words – to conceal as much as we reveal. Words are imprecise, at best, and without great care, become barriers to communication.

In an unpublished transcript of a seminar for young psychiatrists, Sullivan explains how to conduct a history in such a way that communication is maximized and the foundation of a respectful and honest relationship is laid. He suggested to the group:

> Follow the [patient's] account with an attempt to think what you could mean if you were saying that, guided by what you have already learned about a patient. ...that immediately calls up some natural uncertainty, and then ask natural questions to eliminate the uncertainty, so that it gets to be more like an interesting conversation with the patient than a formal history taking. ... This business of trying to keep yourself somewhat in the place where the patient might be and ask the questions that would naturally help you, that is the way to

develop the patient relationship, or one of the most important ways.

Naoko Wake (2006), an historian who has studied Sullivan for a decade, wrote: "As we read verbatim transcripts of his interviews with patients, we find moments when we are not certain whether Sullivan was talking as a doctor or, more simply, as someone who was understanding and willing to listen to, talk to, and learn from others" (p. 327).

Leon Lurie (a student of Sullivan who worked with CC) discussed what he called, "talking from the heart." He believed it took a concerned and skillful therapist to "… create a relationship enabling the participants to speak from the heart, i.e., to have a real 'conversation,' in contrast to the usual exchanges where strategy is the main concern." And what skills does the therapist employ to create such a relationship? Being on the patient's side is certainly one, deep respect another. The willingness to be known is also an essential component.

Self-Revelation

Interpersonal psychotherapy involves both knowing and being known. Several years ago, the popular analyst, Nancy McWilliams' (2004), penned a book on *Psychoanalytic Psychotherapy*. She wrote, "As several analysts have commented in recent years, we try to be our 'best self' with our patients, not our whole self" (p. 39). Lurie maintained that, "… if you feel free to show your worst side, you are showing your better side. Your acceptance of all of yourself is an example to the patient of how he might come to accept himself too" (Frederickson 2005, p. 4). McWilliams' and Lurie's definitions are two ends of a continuum. I believe that Sullivan's intellectual forebear, Ralph Waldo Emerson, saw the situation realistically. He wrote in *Self-Reliance*: "We pass for what we are. Character teaches above our wills. Men imagine that they communicate their virtue or vice only by overt actions, and do not see that virtue or vice emit a breath every moment."

So, perhaps, however unwilling we may be to acknowledge it, there is really no option but to be known by others with whom we are in close relationships. Those who would dismiss Emerson's observation as being naïve because he had no conception of transference might be surprised by another of his observations in the essay, *Experience*: "Temperament also enters fully into the system of illusions [that we maintain about the world], and shuts us in a prison of glass which we cannot see. There is an optical illusion about every person we meet."

So, do we choose to be in an intimate relationship with a patient or *pretend* to be in an intimate relationship? Is our life and our functioning

– including that which patient's see and we do not – available for discussion? This question of what's available for discussion is crucial because far too many patients have had lives full of being told what they could perceive and what they could not.

Otto Will (1971a) wrote:

> The child needs the parent – for shelter, food, protection, education, and affection. Behavior which might interfere seriously with the meeting of such needs must be ignored (dissociated), or "explained away." Thus cruelty may be described as evidence of love, perpetrated for the child's good. (pp. 208-209; this article was also reprinted in the *International Journal of Psychiatry* in 1972).

Borrowing a concept from R.D. Laing (1967, pp.57-76) called *mystification*, Edgar Levenson (2018) put it another way: "The child learns to not know what it knows it knows; that is, she is essentially talked out of her perceptions." He continues, "Mystification, then, is the gap between what is said and what is shown" (p. 173). Many of our patients have been "loved" nearly to death – physically and psychologically. Whether they can articulate it or not at the outset, they are seeking *real* love.

Final Thoughts: A Note about Friendship

The anthropologist, Edward Hall (1992), recounts in his memoirs an instance of David Rioch, Sullivan's colleague, addressing a group of analysts. According to Hall, Rioch began his remarks with this comment: "If people had friends, you fellows would soon be out of business" (p. 232).

On occasion I (CC) have heard colleagues rush to dismiss friendship as having nothing to do with psychotherapy. Indeed, one once said, "I wouldn't want *any* of my clients as friends." What crossed my mind was how different our experiences in therapy must be. I cannot help but think that this colleague's experiences must be less satisfying than *most* of mine have been. I also had two other thoughts: The first was: 'I hope that you don't think that's a secret from your clients' and the second: 'I wonder how they feel about not being good enough to be your friend?'

I have also heard colleagues dismiss the idea of friendship from psychotherapy with a comparison to prostitution or "paid friendship." Critics of psychotherapy often level such a charge: Why should people have to pay for friendship, something that they can get for free? Havens (1989) addressed this issue, as he admitted, defensively, in this way:

> If friendship were not so often paid
> for in ways far more costly than

psychotherapy – as when friends turn out to be predatory enemies – those critics could not be silenced. But as soon as one demands of friendship mutual respect and some happy resonance of interests and styles, there should be no surprise at its rarity or the occasional good sense of paying for it (p. 15).

Later, Havens (1994) returned to the subject of friendship, describing it as a unification of two qualities: closeness and openness (p. 31). He wrote: "Friendship is seen as a model: for psychotherapy, for relationships with oneself or others (for example, the so-called I-thou), and in sexuality, society, and marriage" (p. 36).

Emerson described friendship as having two essential qualities – one is truth, the other tenderness (a word Sullivan used generously). In his essay, *Friendship*, Emerson wrote of the first of these, "A friend is a person with whom I may be sincere. Before him I may think aloud." Who of us should be ashamed to say that we are a friend to our patients?

Reflections

REFERENCES

Blitsten, D. (1966). Unpublished Manuscript. (The authors are grateful to Marisa Shaari, archivist of the Dorothy Blitsten Papers at The Oskar Diethelm Library, DeWitt Wallace Institute for the History of Psychiatry, Weill Cornell Medical College, for making this material available).

Bruch, H. (1974). *Learning Psychotherapy: Rationale and Ground Rules.* Cambridge, MA: Harvard.

Chernin, K. (1995). *A Different Kind of Listening.* New York: HarperCollins.

Cooperman, M. (1987). Some observations regarding psychoanalytic psychotherapy in a hospital setting. *The Psychiatric Hospital, 14,* 21-28.

Erikson, E. (1982). *The Life Cycle Completed: A Review.* New York: W.W. Norton.

Evans, B. (1996). *Harry Stack Sullivan: Interpersonal theory and psychotherapy.* New York: Routledge.

Frederickson, J. (2005, Fall). Jon Frederickson interviews Leon Lurie after sixty years of teaching. *Washington School of Psychiatry News*, 4.

Fromm-Reichmann, F. (1950). *Principles of Intensive Psychotherapy*. Chicago: University of Chicago.

Grosz, S. (2013). *The Examined Life: How we Lose and Find Ourselves*. New York: W.W. Norton.

Guntrip, H. (1971). *Psychoanalytic Theory, Therapy, and the Self*. New York: BasicBooks.

Hall, E. (1992). *An Anthropology of Everyday Life: An Autobiography*. New York: Doubleday.

Havens, L (1976). *Participant Observation*. New York: Jason Aronson.

_____. (1979). Harry Stack Sullivan's contribution to clinical method. *McLean Hospital Journal*, *4*, 20-32.

_____. (1989). *A Safe Place: Laying the Groundwork of Psychotherapy*. Cambridge, MA: Harvard University.

_____. (1994). *Learning to be Human*. Reading, MA: Addison-Wesley.

Kay, J. (2012). In pursuit of emotional security. *Psychiatry*, *75*, 18-21.

Laing, R. (1967). *The Politics of Experience*. New York: Pantheon Books.

Levenson, E. (2017). The interpersonal (Sullivanian) model. In A. Slomowitz (Ed.), *The Purloined Self: Interpersonal Perspectives in Psychoanalysis* (pp. 156-171). New York: Routledge.

Levenson, E. (2018). The enigma of the transference. In A. Slomowitz (Ed.), *Interpersonal Psychoanalysis and the Enigma of Consciousness* (pp. 161-177). New York: Routledge.

Lurie, L. (2008). Theories are ideas. In G. Saiger, S. Rubenfeld, & M. Dluhy (Eds.) *Windows into Today's Group Therapy* (pp. 173-176). New York: Routledge.

McWilliams, N. (2004). *Psychoanalytic Psychotherapy: A Practitioner's Guide.* New York: Guilford.

Richardson, R. (1995). *Emerson: The Mind on Fire.* Berkeley, CA: University of California.

Rioch, D. (1985). Recollections of Harry Stack Sullivan and of the development of his interpersonal psychiatry. *Psychiatry, 48,* 141-158.

Rubin, J. (2014). Each individual is a surprise: A conversation with Marianne Horney Eckardt. *The American Journal of Psychoanalysis, 74,* 115-122.

Sapolsky, R. (2017). *Behave.* New York: Penguin.

Searles, H. (1979). *Countertransference and Related Subjects: Selected Papers.* New York: International Universities Press.

Siegel, D. (2015). *The Developing Mind*; 2nd Edition. New York: Guilford.

Sullivan, H. (1949). The theory of anxiety and the nature of psychotherapy. *Psychiatry*, *12*, 3-12.

_____. (1950). The illusion of personal individuality. *Psychiatry*, *13*, 317-332.

_____. (1953a). *Conceptions of Modern Psychiatry*. New York: W. W. Norton.

_____. (1953b). *The Interpersonal Theory of Psychiatry*. New York: W. W. Norton.

_____. (1954). *The Psychiatric Interview*. New York: W. W. Norton.

_____. (1962). *Schizophrenia as a Human Process*. New York: W.W. Norton.

Stern, D. (2017). Interpersonal psychoanalysis: history and current status. In D. Stern & I. Hirsch (Eds.). *The Interpersonal Perspective in Psychoanalysis, 1960s-1990s* (pp. 1-28). New York: Routledge.

Symington, N. (2006). *A Healing Conversation: How Healing Happens*. London: Karnac.

_____. (2012). *The Psychology of the Person*. London: Karnac.

Wake, N. (2006). The full story by no means told: Harry Stack Sullivan at Sheppard-Pratt, 1922-1930. *History of Psychology*, *9*, 325-358.

White, W. (1938). *The Autobiography of a Purpose.* New York: Arno Press.

Will, O. (1949, February 6). The career of Dr. Harry Stack Sullivan: D. C. doctor pitted psychiatry against war. *The Washington Post*, B5.

_____. (1954). Introduction. In H. Sullivan, *The Psychiatric Interview* (pp. ix-xxii). New York: Norton.

_____. (1962). Hallucinations: comments reflecting clinical observations of the schizophrenic reaction. In L. West (Ed.), *Hallucinations* (pp. 174-182). New York: Grune & Stratton.

_____. (1963, March). The awareness of need and the schizophrenic reaction. Presented at the Fortieth Annual Meeting of the American Orthopsychiatric Association, Washington, DC.

_____. (1965). The beginning of psychotherapeutic experience. In A. Burton (Ed.), *Modern Psychotherapeutic Practice* (pp. 3-35). Palo Alto, CA: Science & Behavior Books.

_____. (1968). Schizophrenia and psychotherapy. In J. Marmor (Ed.), *Modern Psychoanalysis: New Directions and Perspectives* (pp. 551-573).New York: Basic Books.

_____. (1970a). The relationship of schizophrenia to psychotherapy. *Journal of Private Psychiatric Hospitals, 2*, 18-24.

_____. (1970b). The therapeutic use of self. *Medical Arts & Sciences*, *24*, 3-14.

_____. (1971a). Commentary [on the article Paranoia or persecution: the case of Schreber by M. Schatzman]. *Family Process*, *10*, 207-210.

_____. (1971b). The patient and the psychotherapist: Comments on the "uniqueness" of their relationship. In B. Landis & E. Tauber (Eds.), *In the Name of Life: Essays in Honor of Erich Fromm* (15-43). New York, NY: Holt, Rinehart & Winston.

_____. (1972). Commentary on Paranoia or persecution: the case of Schreber by Morton Schatzman. *International Journal of Psychiatry*, *10*, 85-88.

_____. (1975). The conditions of being therapeutic. In J. G. Gunderson & L. R. Mosher (Eds.). *Psychotherapy of Schizophrenia* (53-66). New York, NY: Jason Aronson.

_____. (1979a). Comments on the professional life of the psychotherapist. *Contemporary Psychoanalysis*, *15*, 560-576.

_____. (1979b). On "caring" in psychotherapy. Unpublished Manuscript. (The authors are grateful to Joel Kanter, LCSW, for making this material available from his personal archive).

_____. (1980). Comments on the "elements" of schizophrenia, psychotherapy, and the schizophrenic person. In J. Strauss, et al (Eds.). *The Psychotherapy of Schizophrenia* (pp. 157-166). New York: Plenum.

_____. (1981). Memories of Harry Stack Sullivan. Unpublished Manuscript. (The authors are grateful to Joel Kanter, LCSW, for making this material available from his personal archive).

_____. (1983). Foreward. In J. G. Gunderson, O. A. Will, & L. R. Mosher (Eds.). *Principles and Practice of Milieu Therapy* (vii-x). New York, NY: Jason Aronson.

_____. (1987). Illuminations of the human condition. In J. Sacksteder, D. Schwartz, & Y. Akabane (Eds.), *Attachment and the Therapeutic Process: Essays in Honor of Otto Allen Will, Jr.* (pp. 241-261). Madison, CT: International Universities Press.

_____. (1989). In memory of Frieda. In A. Silver (Ed.), *Psychoanalysis and Psychosis* (131-144). Madison, CT: International Universities Press.

Yeats, W. (1902). *Celtic Twilight*. New York: Bibliobazaar.

Reflections

www.ingramcontent.com/pod-product-compliance
Lightning Source LLC
Chambersburg PA
CBHW030258030426
42336CB00009B/432